MEET SARA . . . AND HER SPOOKY FRIENDS!

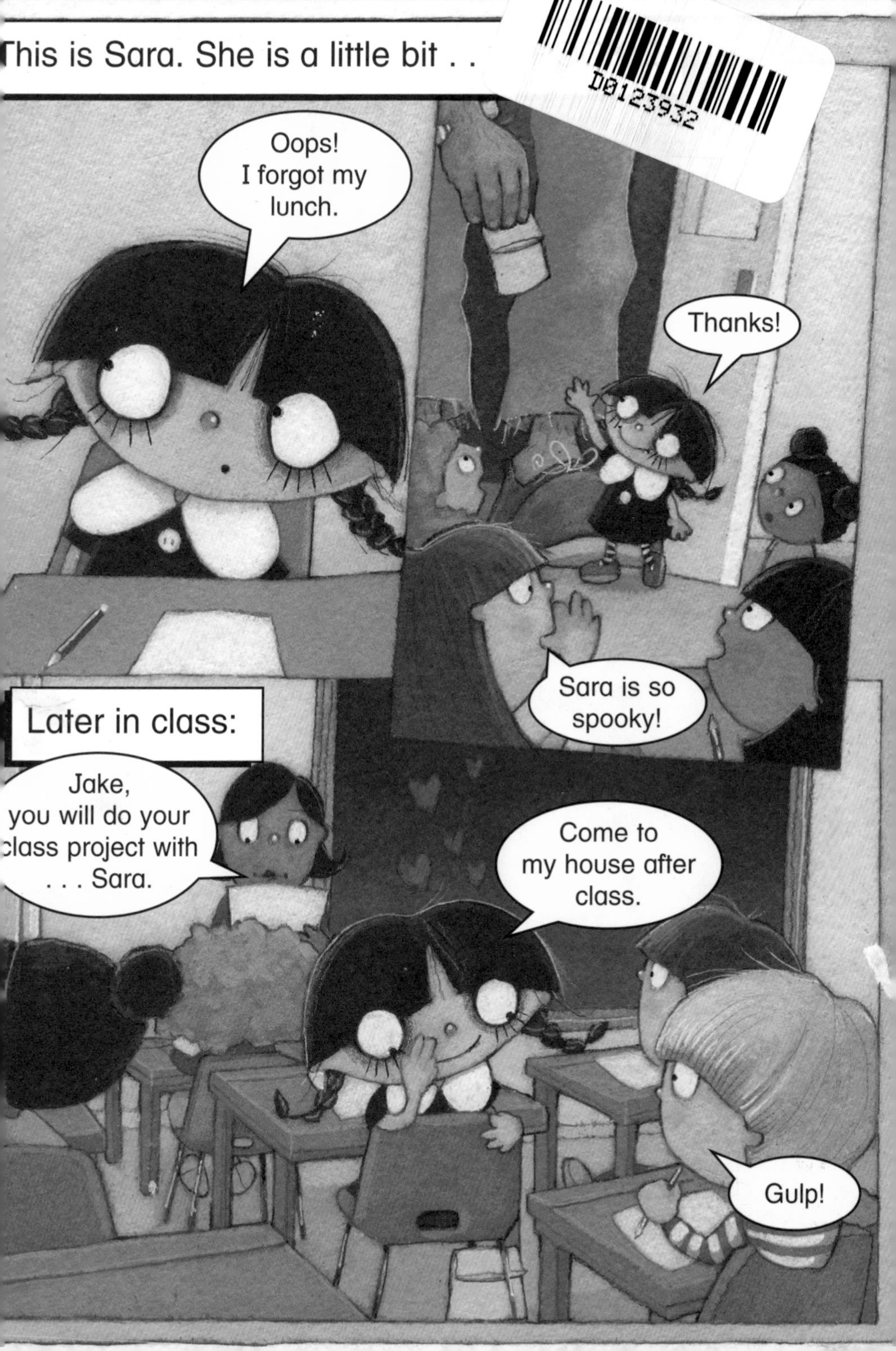
This is Sara. She is a little bit . .
Oops! I forgot my lunch.
Thanks!
Sara is so spooky!
Later in class:
Jake, you will do your class project with . . . Sara.
Come to my house after class.
Gulp!

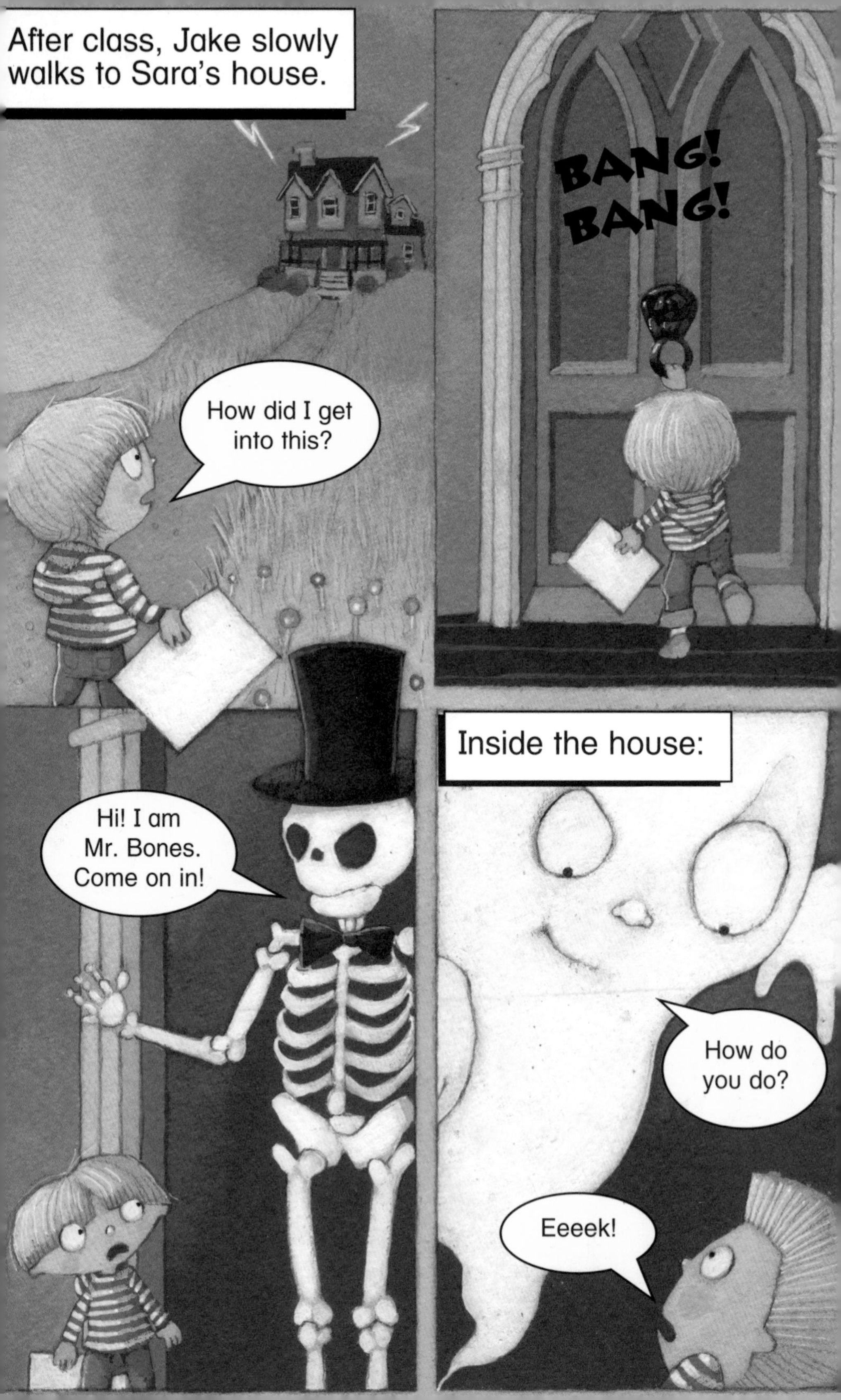
After class, Jake slowly walks to Sara's house.
How did I get into this?
BANG! BANG!
Hi! I am Mr. Bones. Come on in!
Inside the house:
How do you do?
Eeeek!

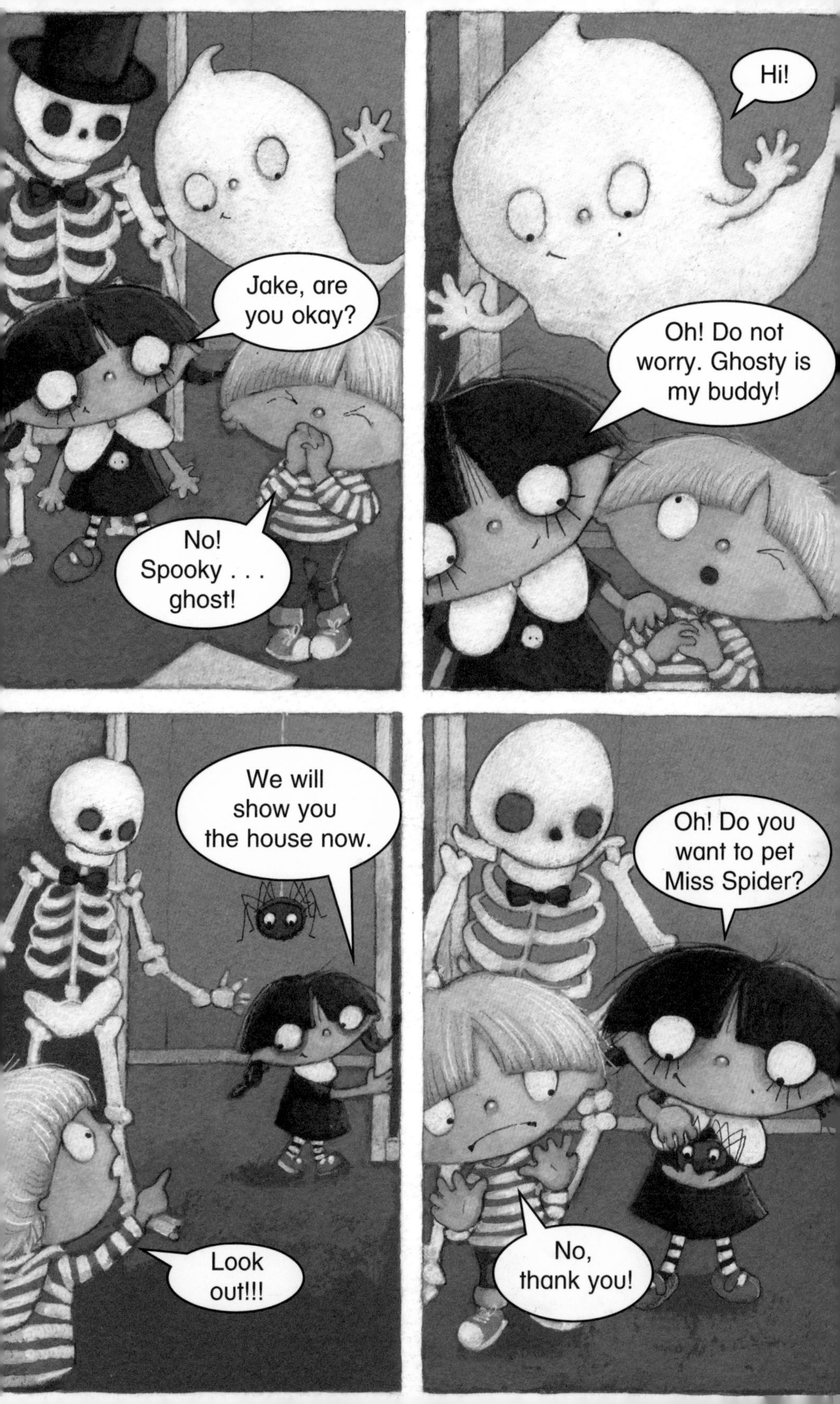
Jake, are you okay?
No! Spooky . . . ghost!
Hi!
Oh! Do not worry. Ghosty is my buddy!
We will show you the house now.
Look out!!!
Oh! Do you want to pet Miss Spider?
No, thank you!

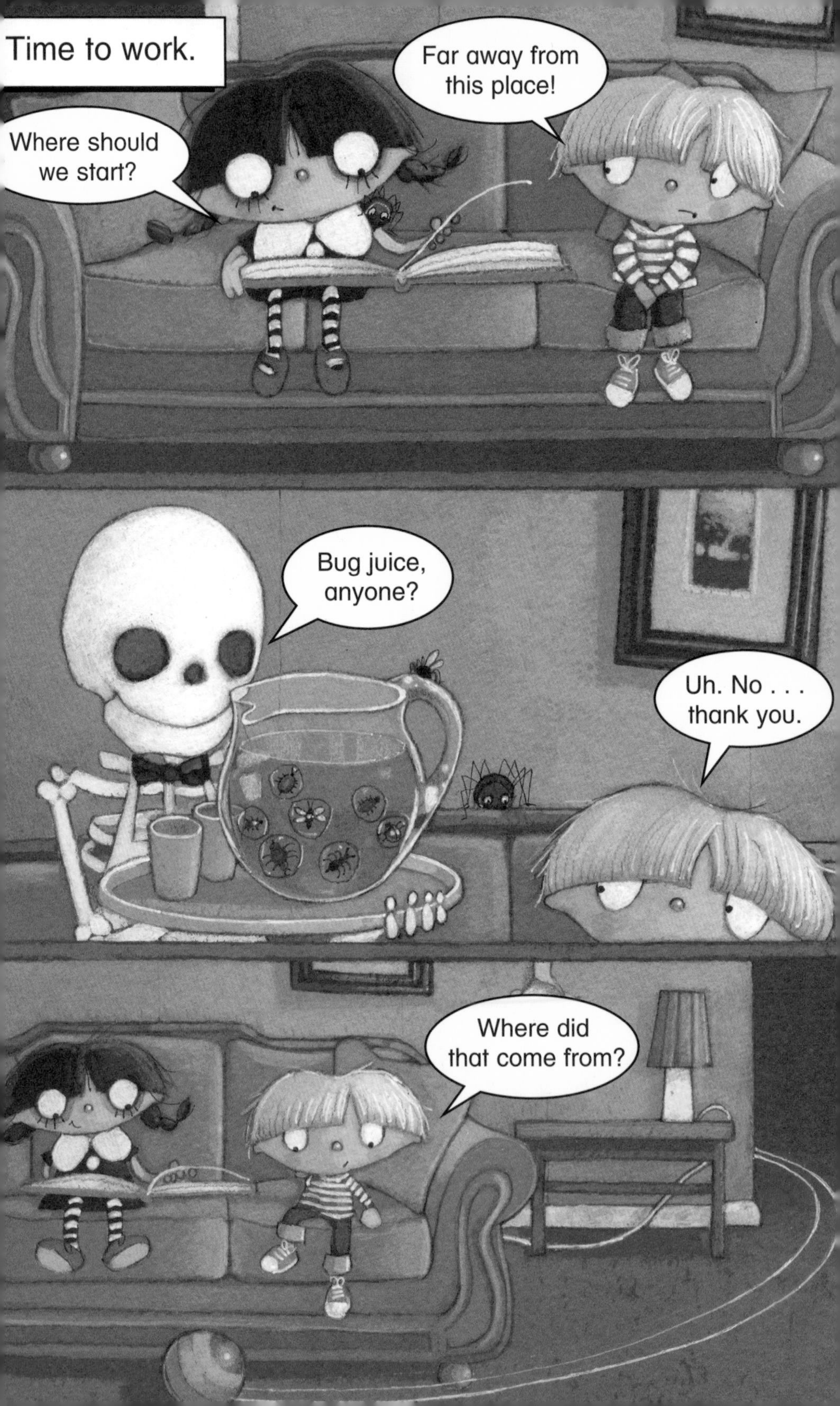
Time to work.
Where should we start?
Far away from this place!
Bug juice, anyone?
Uh. No . . . thank you.
Where did that come from?

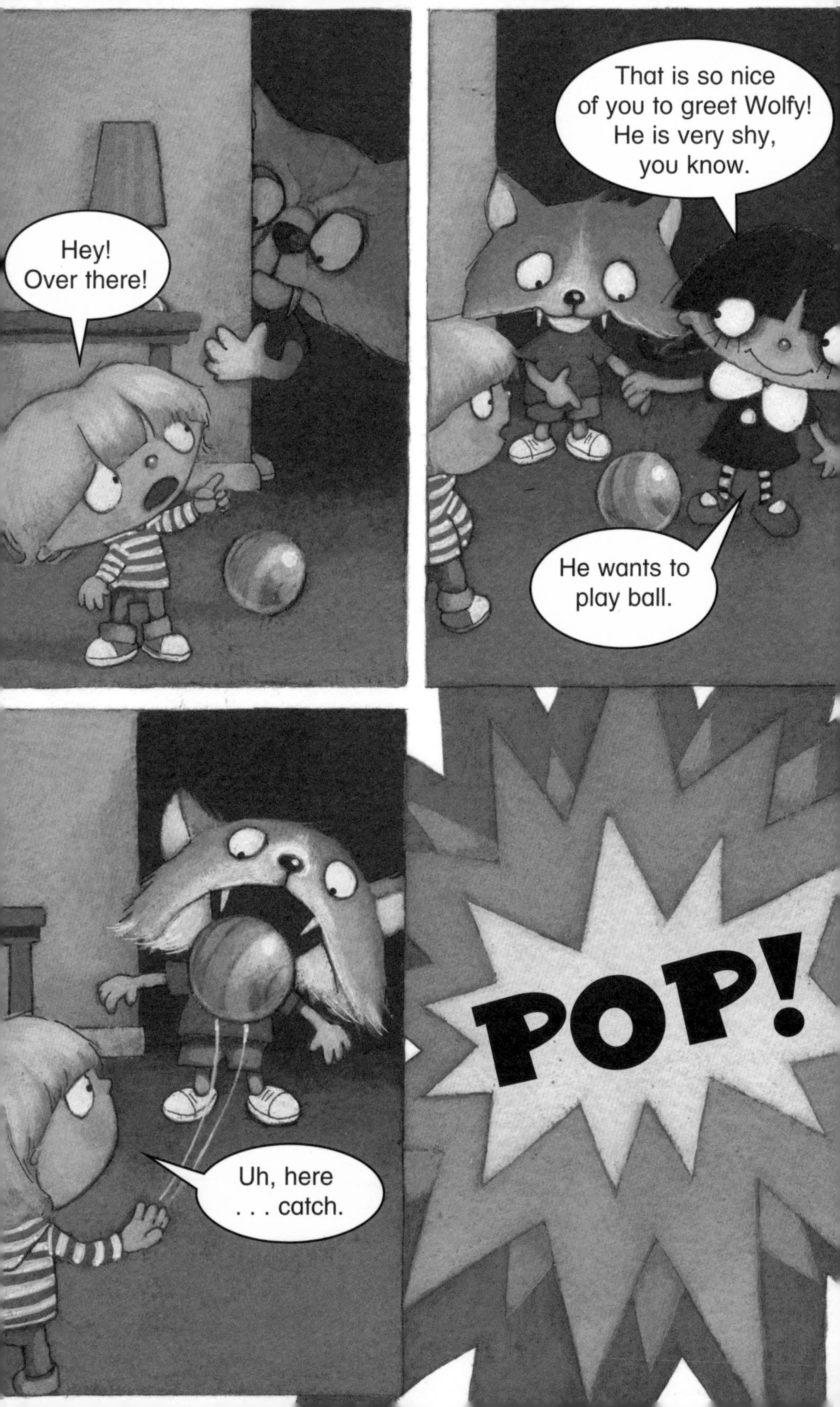
Hey!
Over there!
That is so nice
of you to greet Wolfy!
He is very shy,
you know.
He wants to
play ball.
Uh, here
. . . catch.
POP!

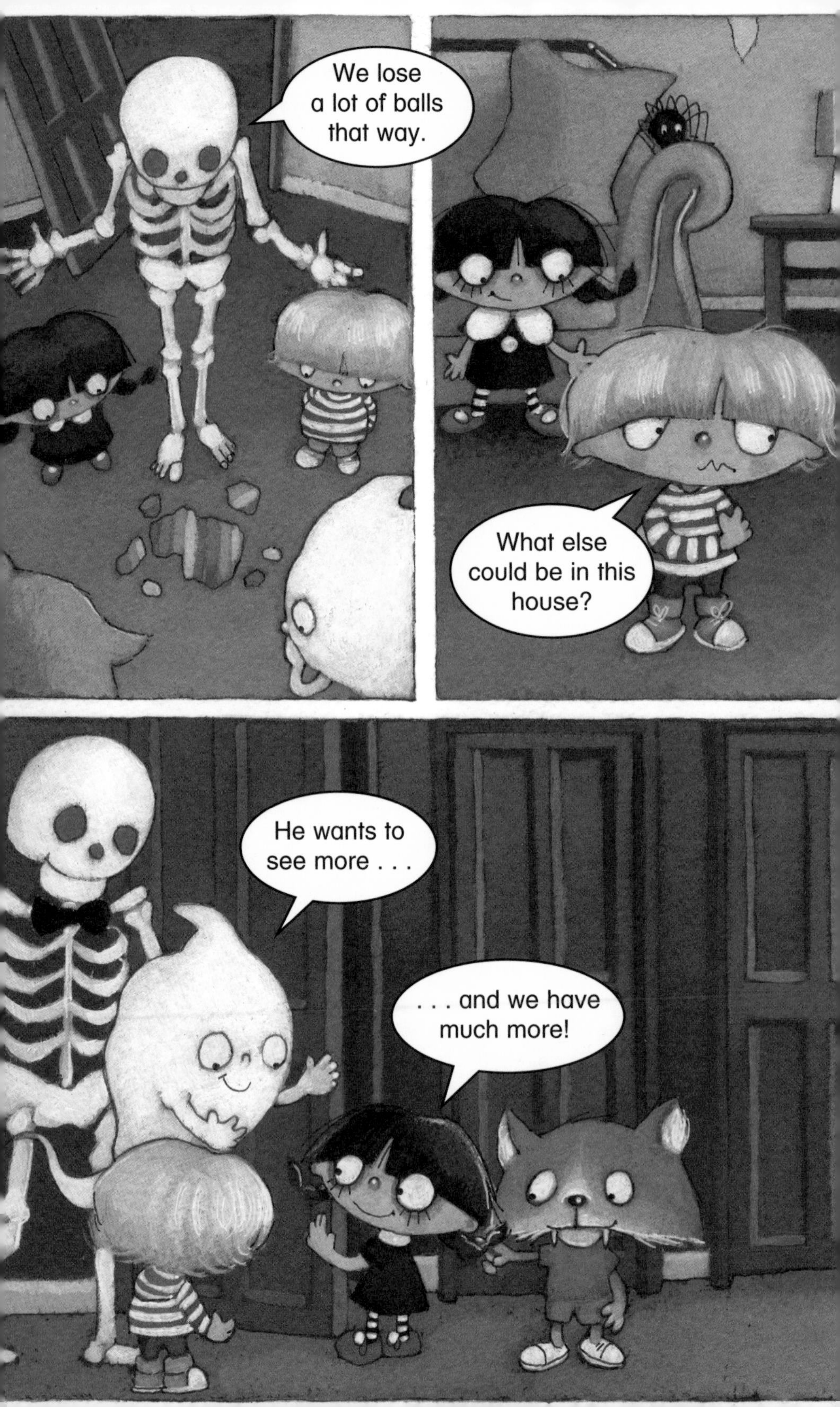

We lose a lot of balls that way.
What else could be in this house?
He wants to see more . . .
. . . and we have much more!

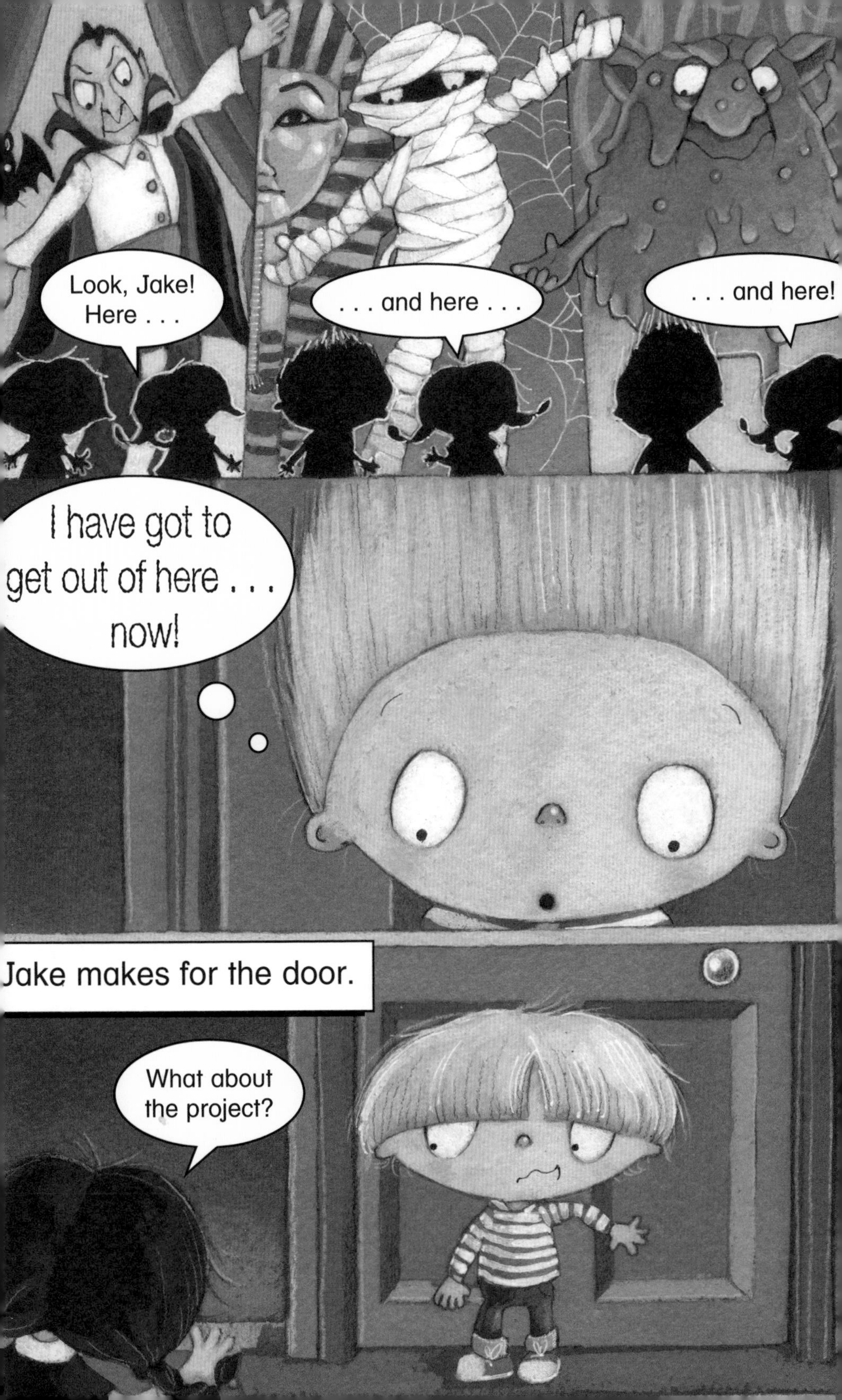
Look, Jake! Here . . .
. . . and here . . .
. . . and here!
I have got to get out of here . . . now!
Jake makes for the door.
What about the project?

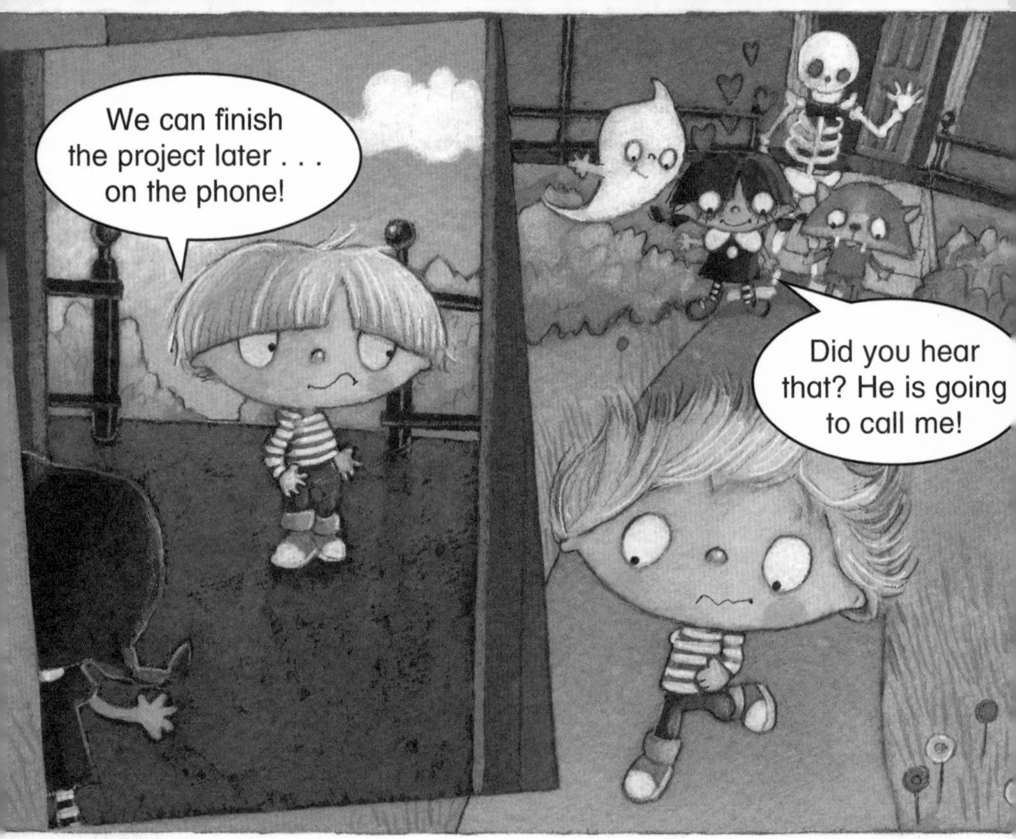

We can finish the project later . . . on the phone!
Did you hear that? He is going to call me!

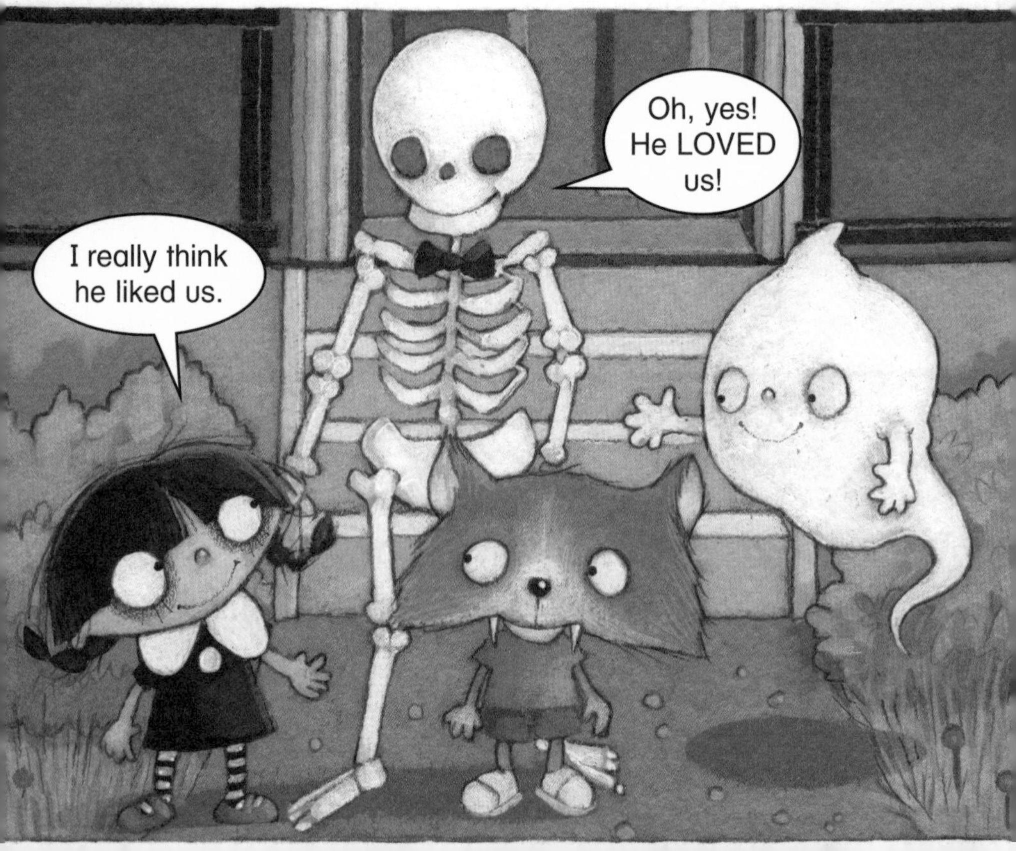

I really think he liked us.
Oh, yes! He LOVED us!

SPOOKY COOKOUT

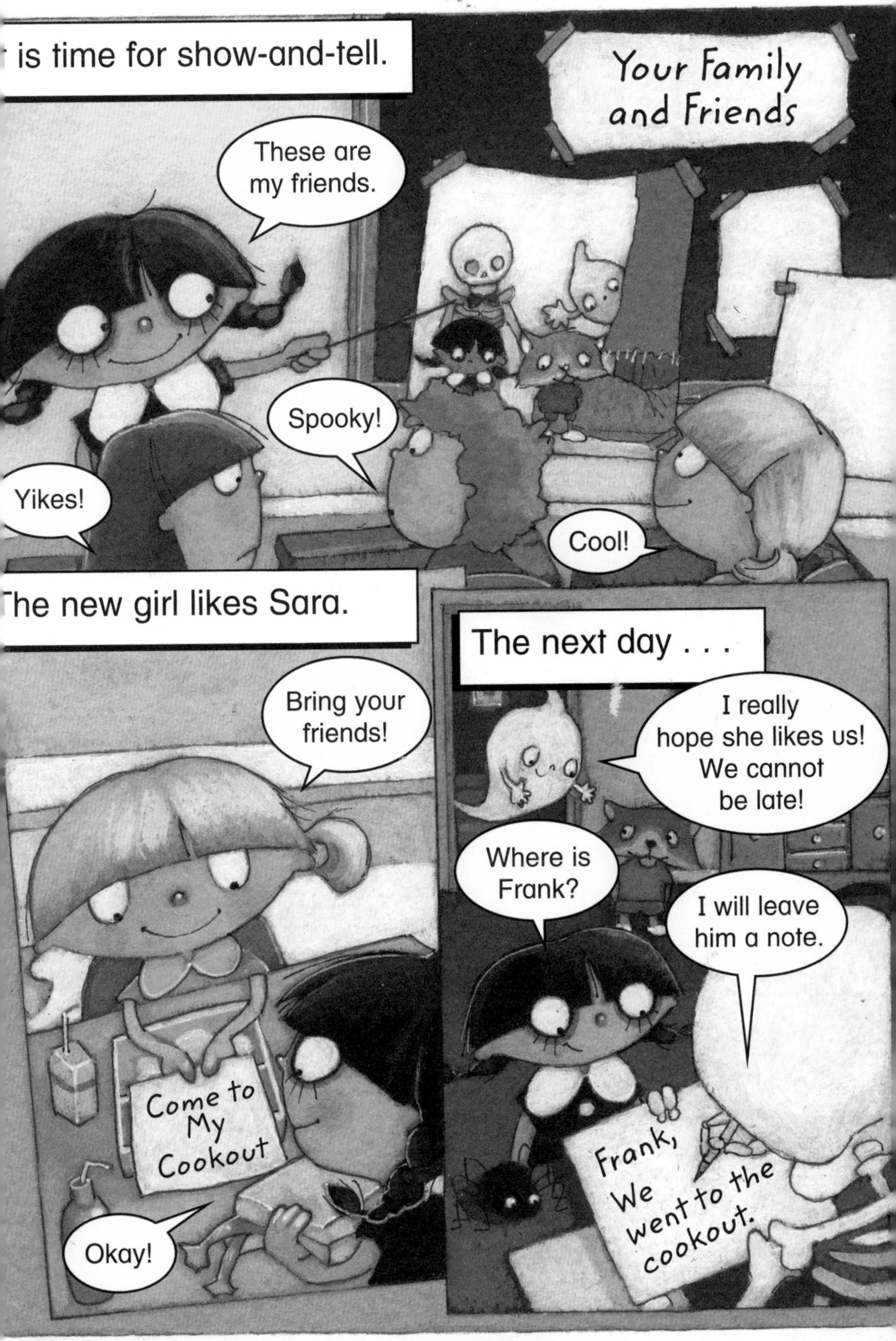

is time for show-and-tell.
Your Family and Friends
These are my friends.
Spooky!
Yikes!
Cool!
The new girl likes Sara.
Bring your friends!
Come to My Cookout
Okay!
The next day . . .
I really hope she likes us! We cannot be late!
Where is Frank?
I will leave him a note.
Frank, We went to the cookout.

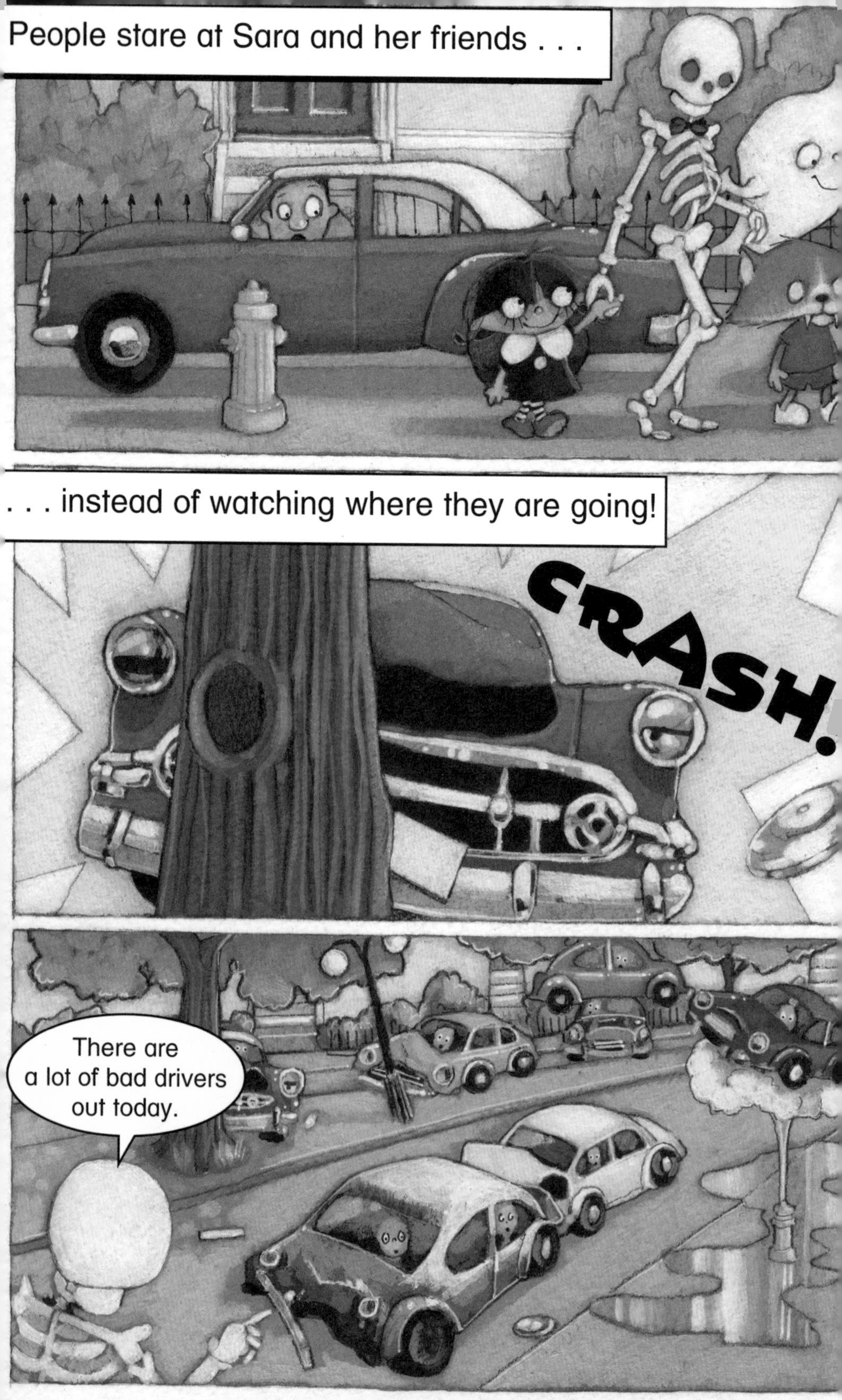
People stare at Sara and her friends . . .
. . . instead of watching where they are going!
CRASH!
There are a lot of bad drivers out today.

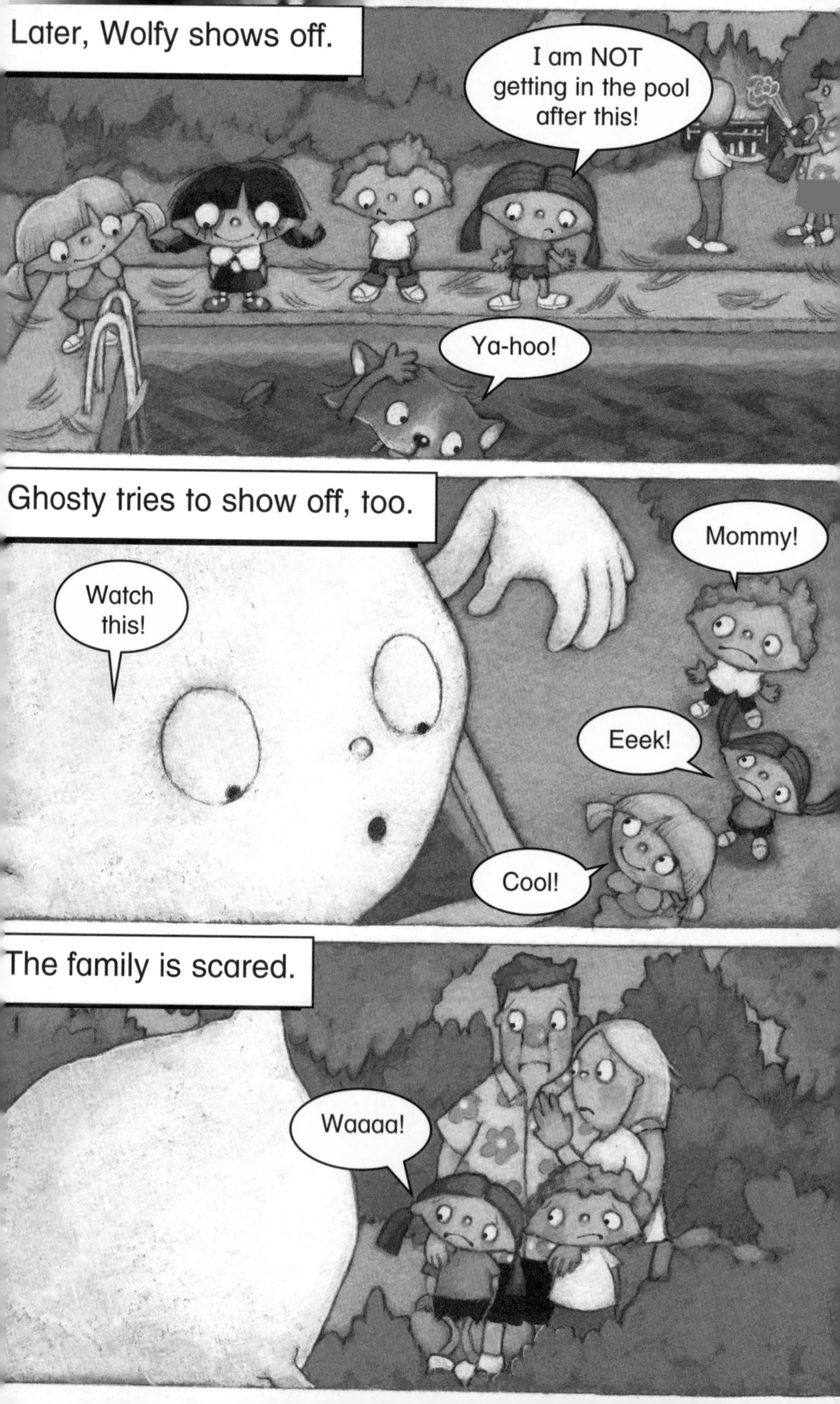
Later, Wolfy shows off.
I am NOT getting in the pool after this!
Ya-hoo!
Ghosty tries to show off, too.
Watch this!
Mommy!
Eeek!
Cool!
The family is scared.
Waaaa!

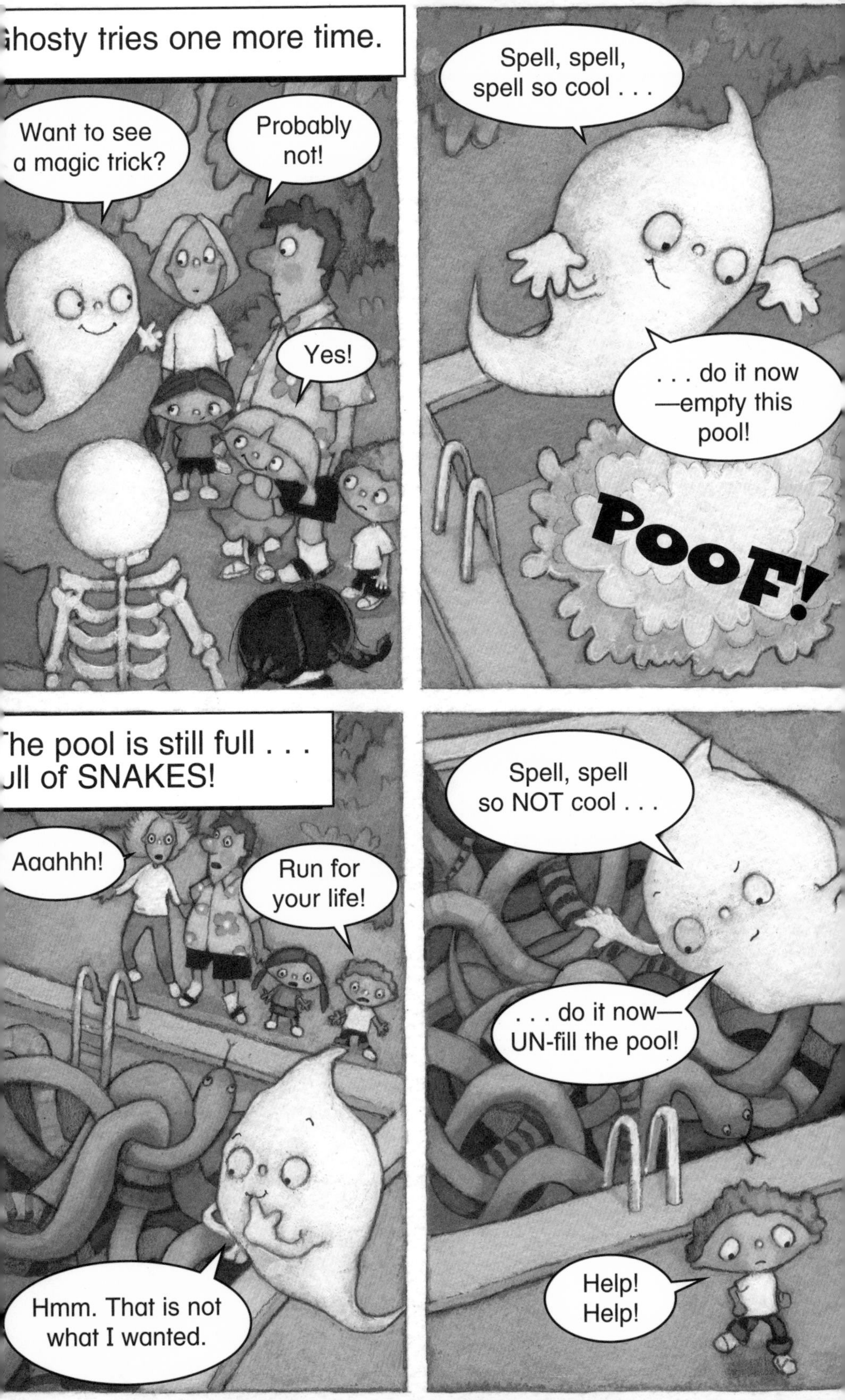
hosty tries one more time.
Want to see a magic trick?
Probably not!
Yes!
Spell, spell, spell so cool . . .
. . . do it now —empty this pool!
POOF!
he pool is still full . . .
ll of SNAKES!
Aaahhh!
Run for your life!
Hmm. That is not what I wanted.
Spell, spell so NOT cool . . .
. . . do it now— UN-fill the pool!
Help! Help!

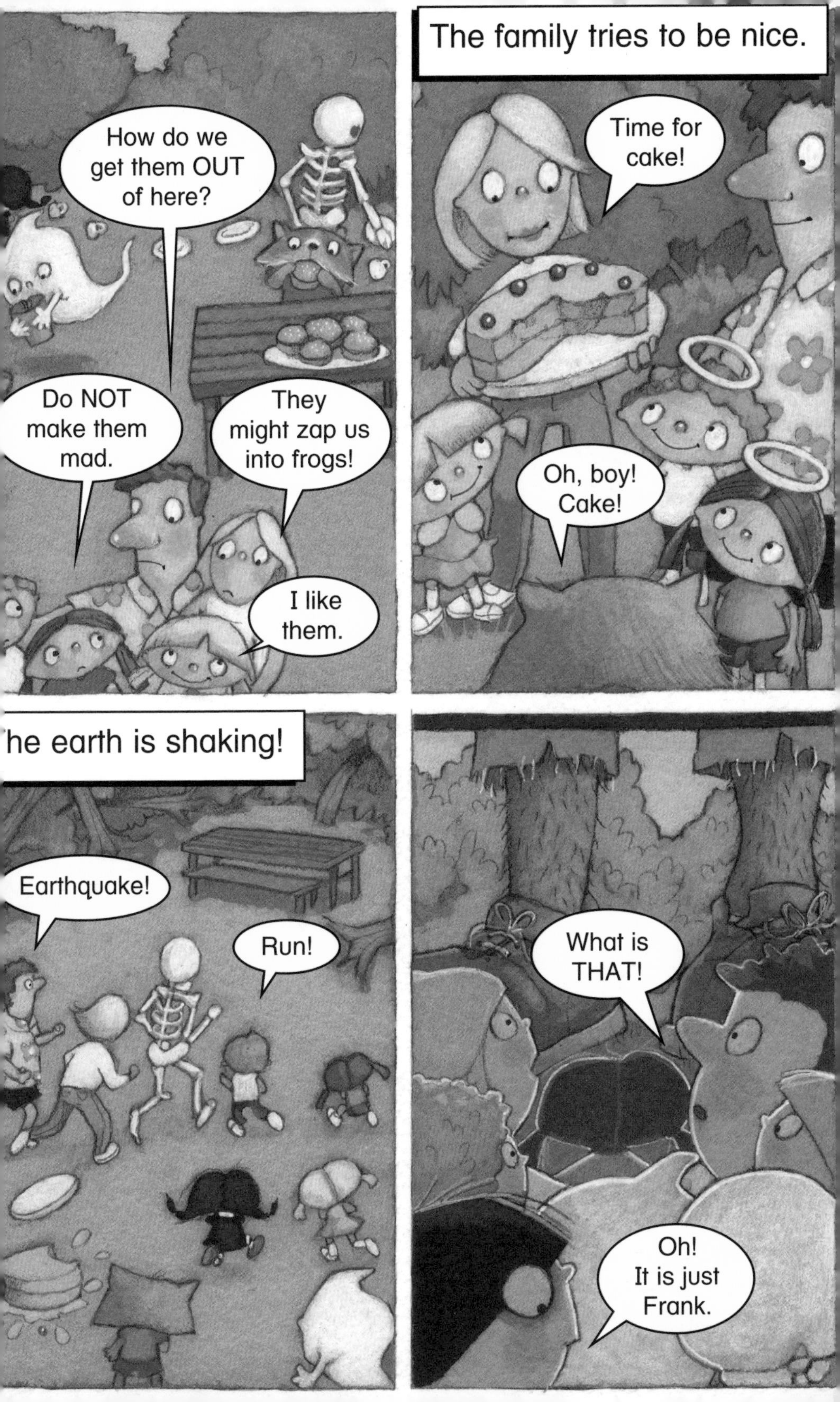
How do we get them OUT of here?
Do NOT make them mad.
They might zap us into frogs!
I like them.
The family tries to be nice.
Time for cake!
Oh, boy! Cake!
he earth is shaking!
Earthquake!
Run!
What is THAT!
Oh! It is just Frank.

A HOWLING SLUMBER PARTY

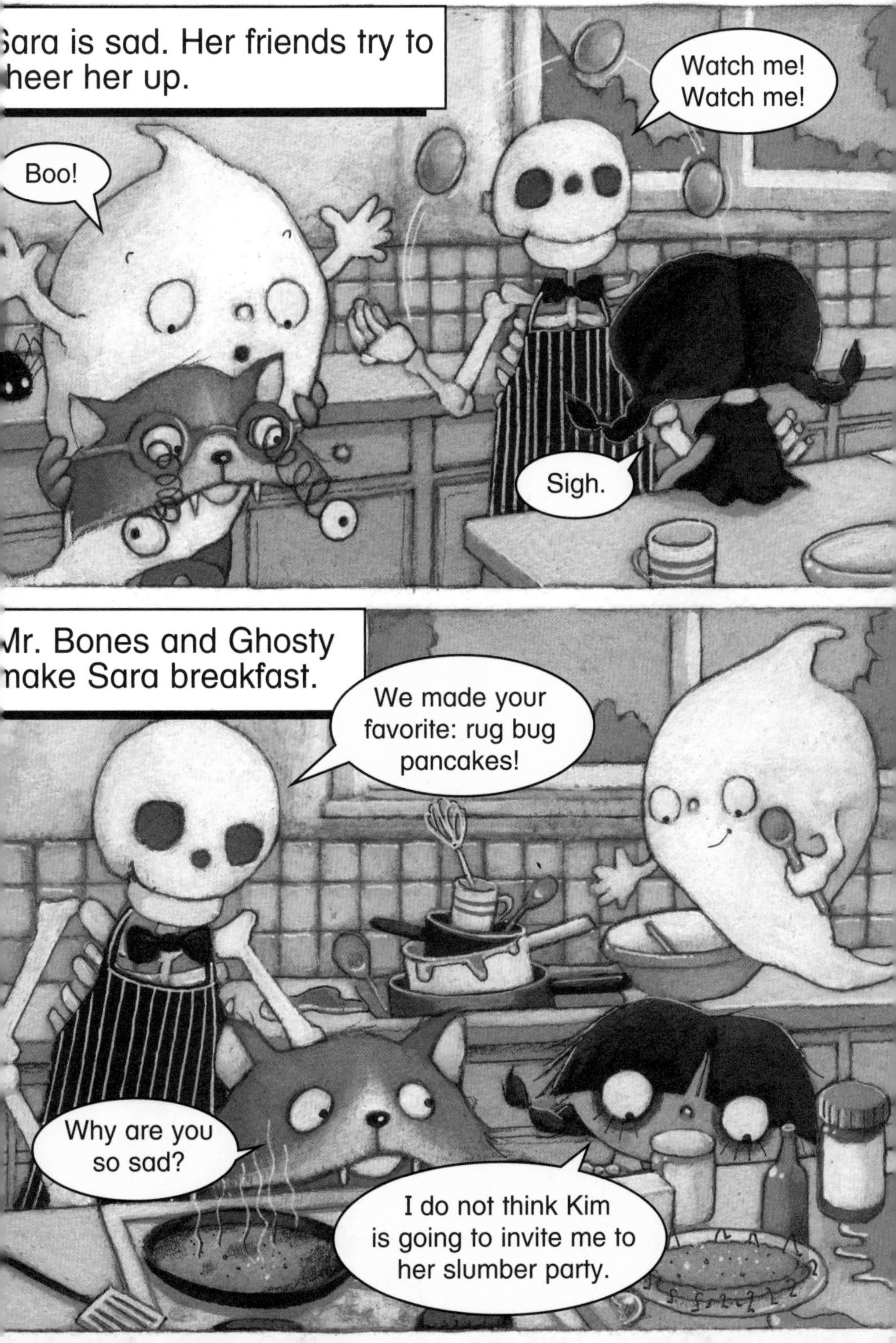
ara is sad. Her friends try to
heer her up.
Boo!
Watch me!
Watch me!
Sigh.
Ir. Bones and Ghosty
nake Sara breakfast.
We made your favorite: rug bug pancakes!
Why are you so sad?
I do not think Kim is going to invite me to her slumber party.

In class that day . . .

Later, Wolfy howls with sadness.

Sara leaves for the party.

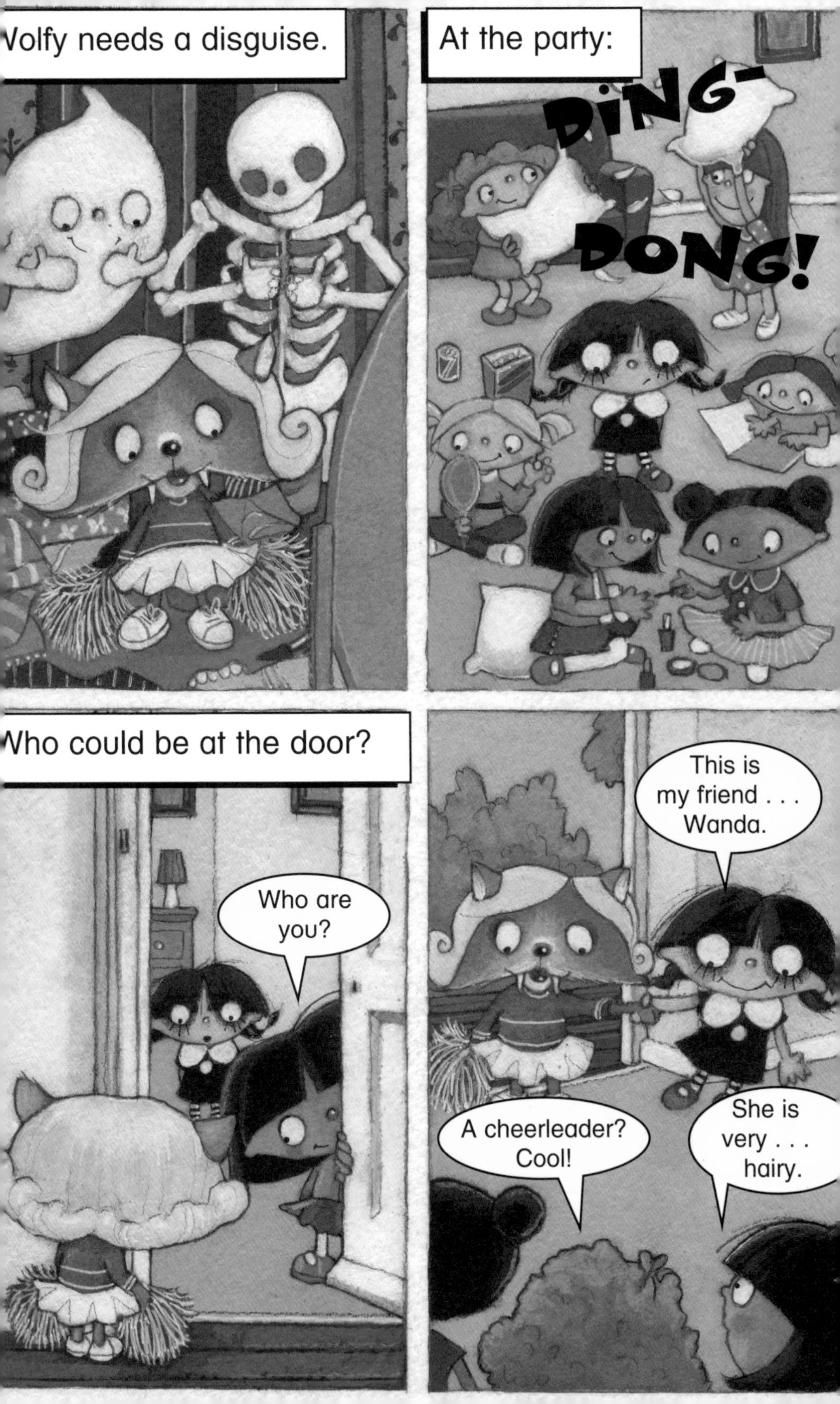

Wolfy needs a disguise.
At the party:
DING-
DONG!
Who could be at the door?
Who are you?
This is my friend . . . Wanda.
A cheerleader? Cool!
She is very . . . hairy.

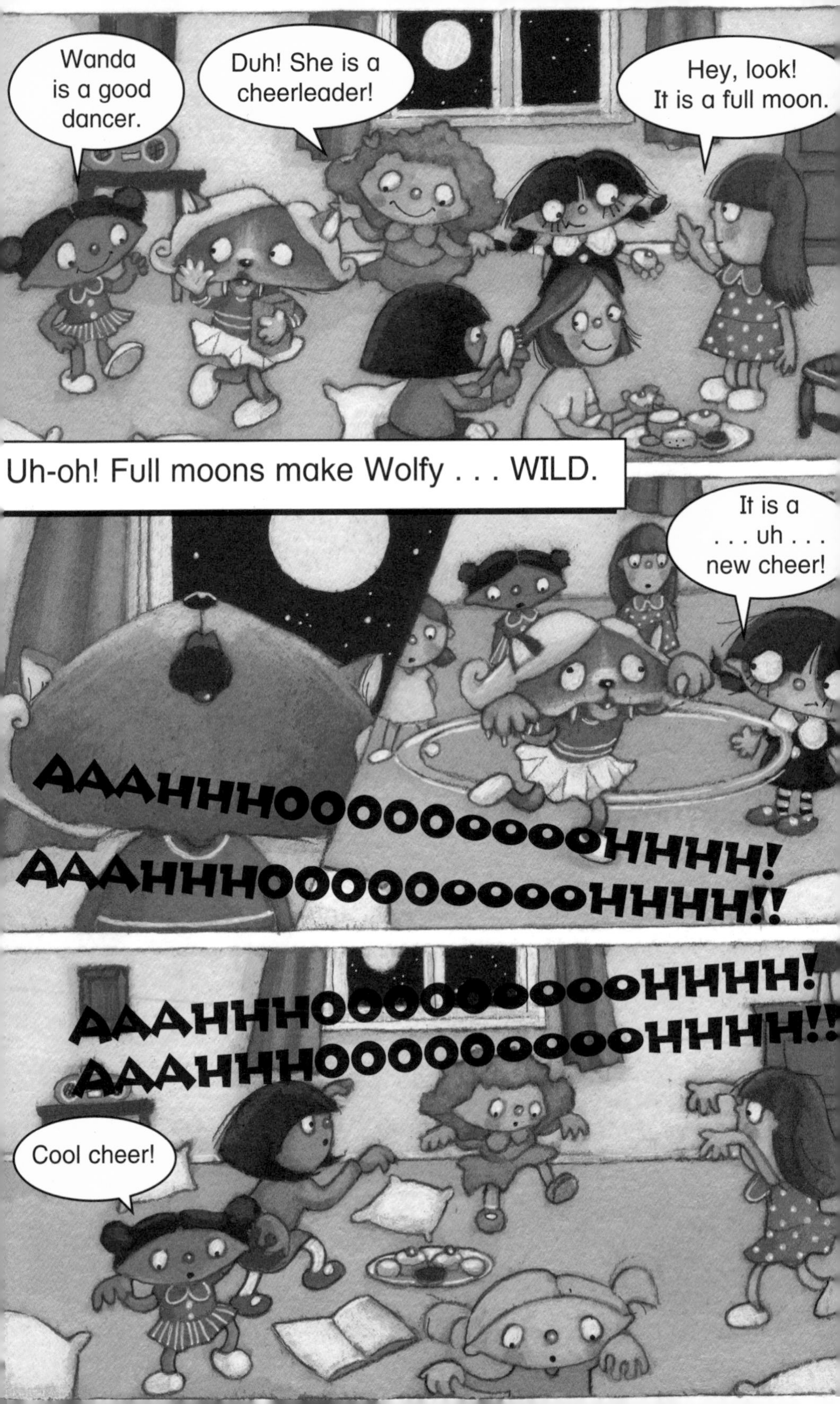
Wanda is a good dancer.
Duh! She is a cheerleader!
Hey, look! It is a full moon.
Uh-oh! Full moons make Wolfy . . . WILD.
It is a . . . uh . . . new cheer!
AAAHHHOOOOOOOOOOOHHHH!
AAAHHHOOOOOOOOOOOHHHH!!
AAAHHHOOOOOOOOOOOHHHH!
AAAHHHOOOOOOOOOOOHHHH!!
Cool cheer!

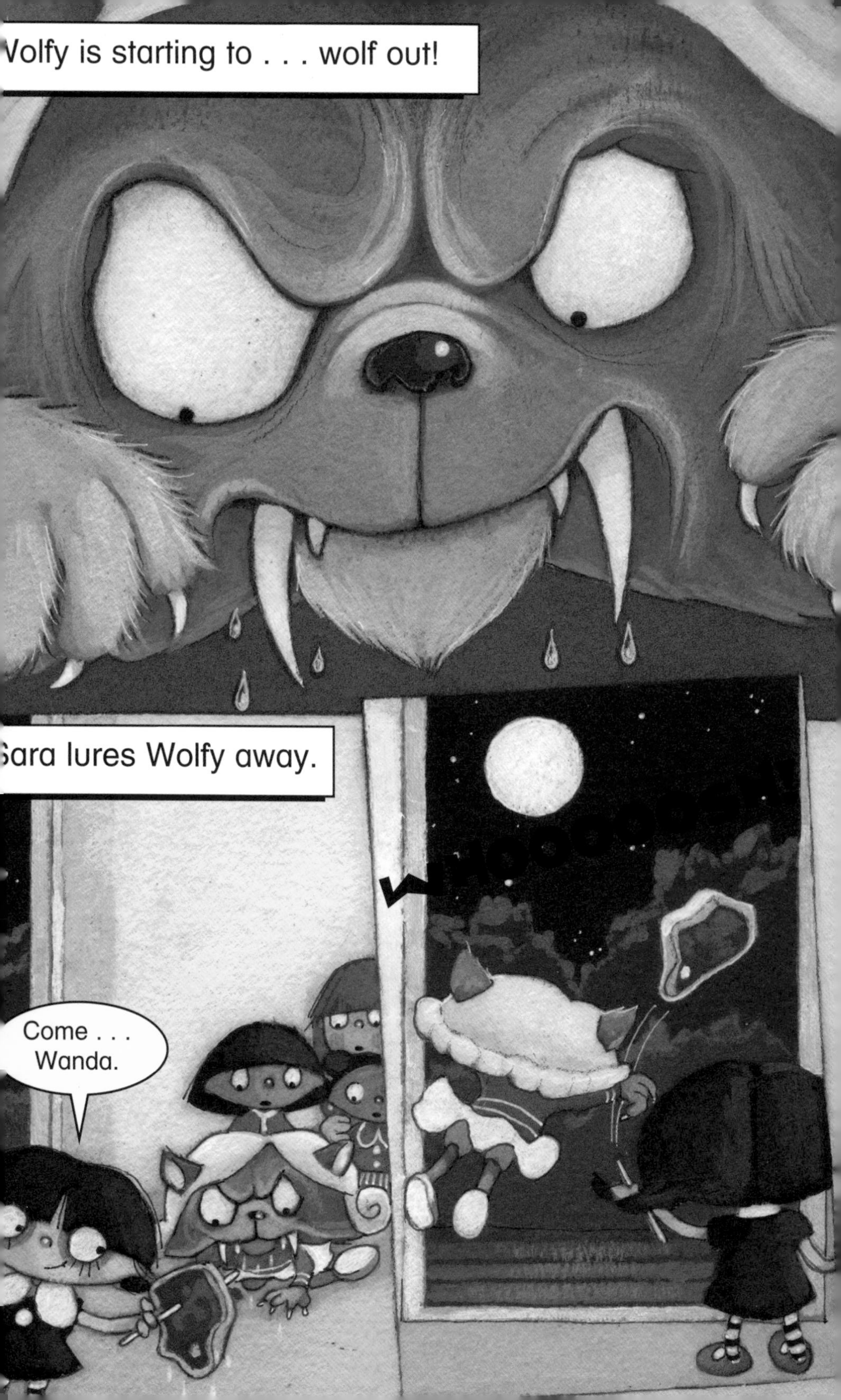
Wolfy is starting to . . . wolf out!
Sara lures Wolfy away.
Come . . . Wanda.

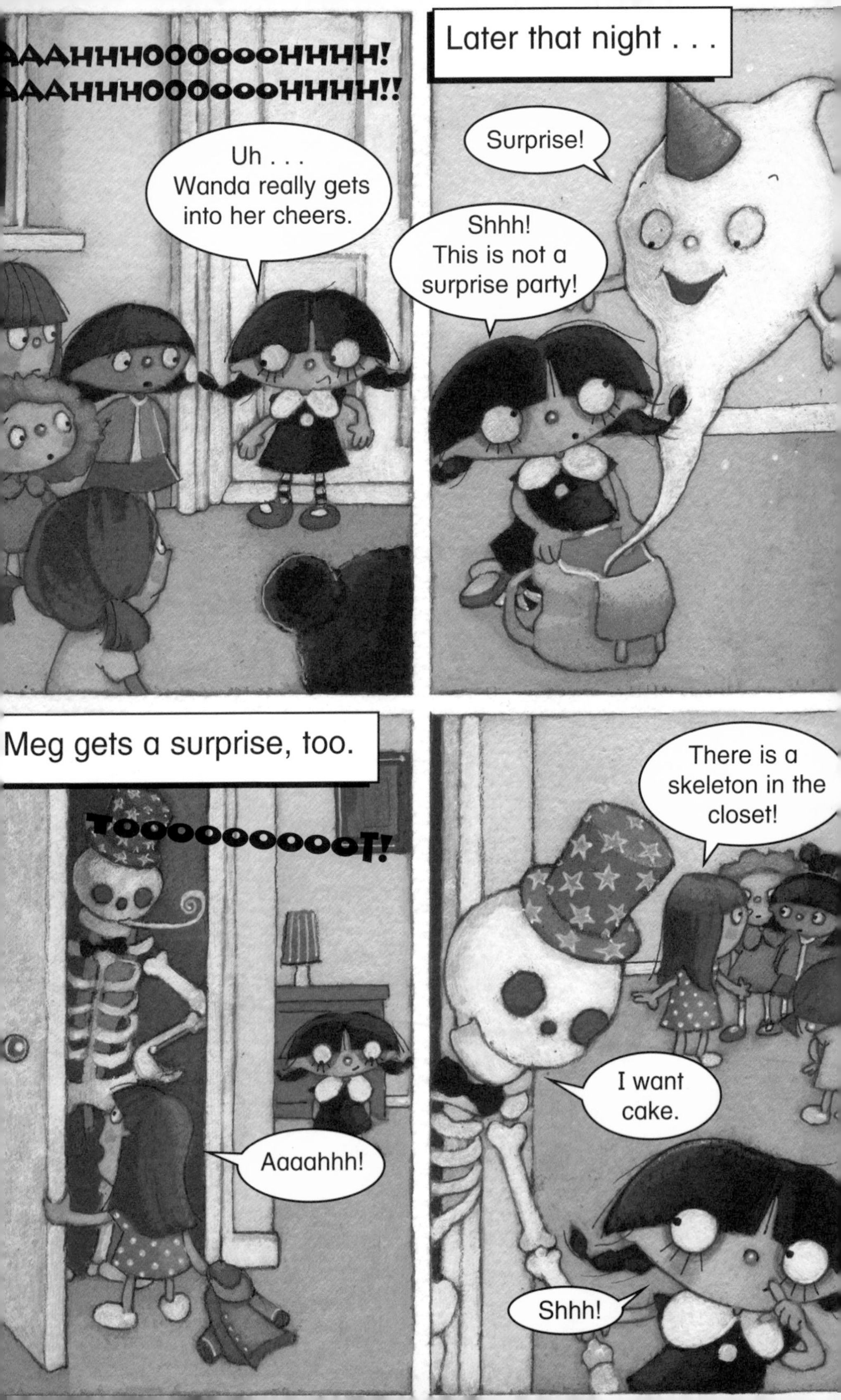
AAAHHHOOOooooHHHH!
AAAHHHOOOooooHHHH!!
Uh . . .
Wanda really gets
into her cheers.
Later that night . . .
Surprise!
Shhh!
This is not a
surprise party!
Meg gets a surprise, too.
TOOOOOOOOOT!
Aaaahhh!
There is a
skeleton in the
closet!
I want
cake.
Shhh!

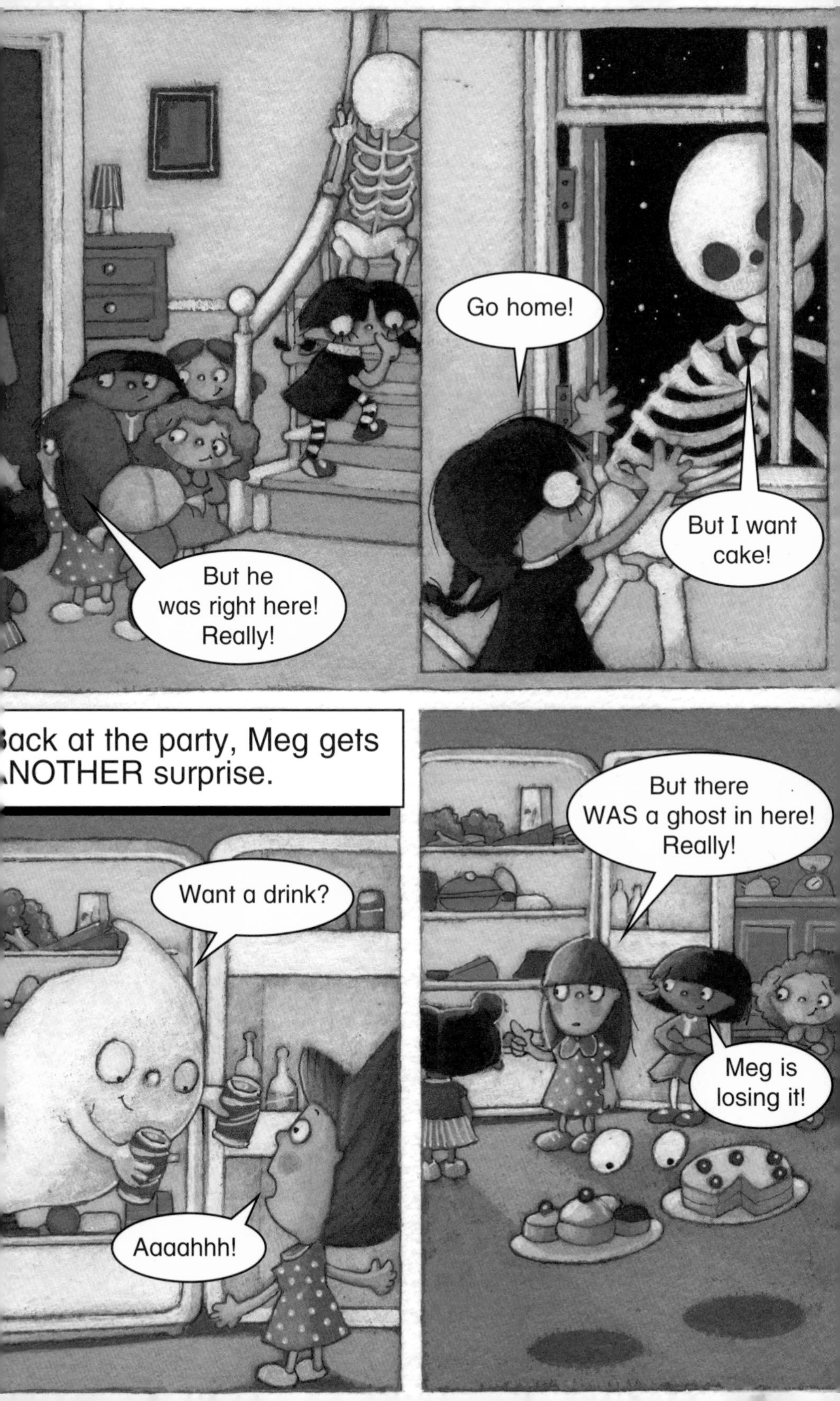
But he was right here! Really!
Go home!
But I want cake!
ack at the party, Meg gets
NOTHER surprise.
Want a drink?
Aaaahhh!
But there WAS a ghost in here! Really!
Meg is losing it!

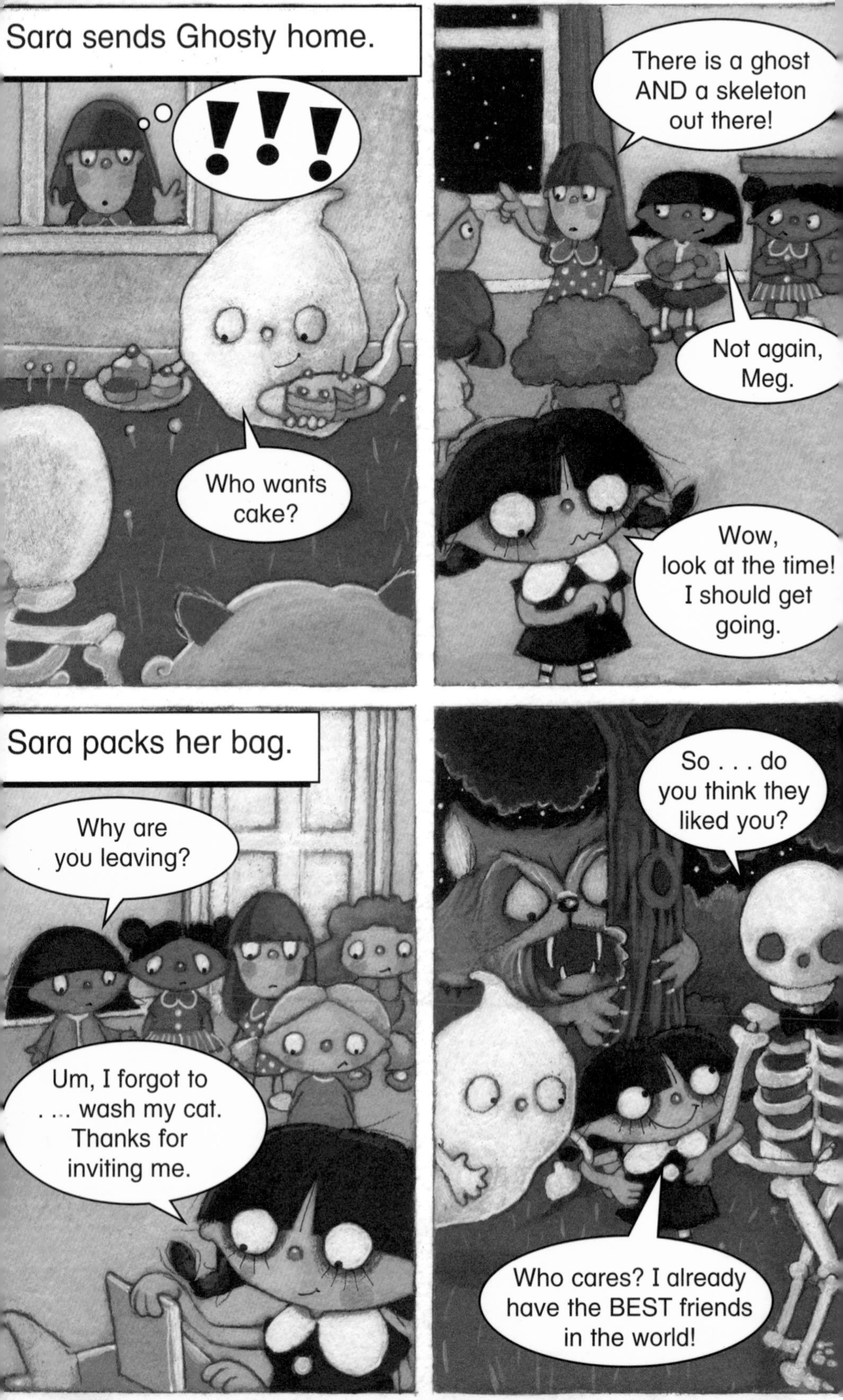
Sara sends Ghosty home.
!!!
Who wants cake?
There is a ghost AND a skeleton out there!
Not again, Meg.
Wow, look at the time! I should get going.
Sara packs her bag.
Why are you leaving?
Um, I forgot to . ... wash my cat. Thanks for inviting me.
So . . . do you think they liked you?
Who cares? I already have the BEST friends in the world!